D1065343

Easy

Origami

Ornaments

An Augmented Reality Crafting Experience

by Christopher Harbo

CAPSTONE PRESS
a capstone imprint

First Facts are published by Capstone Press,
1710 Roe Crest Drive, North Mankato, Minnesota 56003
www.mycapstone.com

Library of Congress Cataloging-in-Publication Data
Library of Congress Cataloging-in-Publication data is
available on the Library of Congress website.
ISBN: 978-1-5157-3586-1 (library binding)
ISBN: 978-1-5157-3591-5 (eBook PDF)

Summary: Provides photo-illustrated instructions for making
five origami models and three craft projects. Also includes
embedded video links for online instructional tutorials that
can be accessed with the Capstone 4D app.

Editorial Credits
Sarah Bennett, designer; Laura Manthe, production specialist

The author thanks Rachel Walwood for designing and
creating all of the origami craft projects in this book.

Photo Credits
Photographs and design elements by Capstone Studio: Karon
Dubke, except Shutterstock: Darren Henry, 18 (boy), 19
(boy), Lorena Fernandez, 18 (girl), 19 (girl). Line drawings
by Capstone: Sandra D'Antonio. Additional design elements:
Shutterstock: Ammak, Lena Bukovsky

Printed in the United States of America.
010077S17

Table of Contents

Outstanding Origami Ornaments

Perfectly folded origami models are a joy to behold. But hang them on strings, and your tiny paper creations become marvelous masterpieces. With a few simple steps, a dozen paper bluebells become beautiful garland for any tree. And two folded photo frames can easily join together for the perfect keepsake ornament. No matter how you hang origami, the only limit to the ornaments you can create is your imagination!

Download the Capstone 4D App!

Videos for every fold and craft are now at your fingertips with the Capstone 4D app.

To download the Capstone 4D app:
• Search in the Apple App Store or Google Play for "Capstone 4D"
• Click *Install* (Android) or *Get*, then *Install* (Apple)
• Open the application
• Scan any page with this icon

You can also access the additional resources on the web at **www.capstone4D.com** using the password **fold.ornament**

Materials

Origami is great for crafting because the materials don't cost much. Below are the basic supplies you'll use to complete the projects in this book.

origami paper

hot glue

clothespins

string

double-sided tape

beads

scissors

photos

sewing needle

craft glue

Terms and Techniques

Folding paper is easier when you understand basic origami folding terms and symbols. Practice the folds below before trying the models in this book.

Valley folds are represented by a dashed line. One side of the paper is folded against the other like a book.

Mountain folds are represented by a dashed and dotted line. The paper is folded sharply behind the model.

Squash folds are formed by lifting one edge of a pocket. The pocket gets folded again so the spine gets flattened. The existing fold lines become new edges.

Inside reverse folds are made by opening a pocket slightly. Then you fold the model inside itself along the fold lines or existing creases.

Outside reverse folds are made by opening a pocket slightly. Then you fold the model outside itself along the fold lines or existing creases.

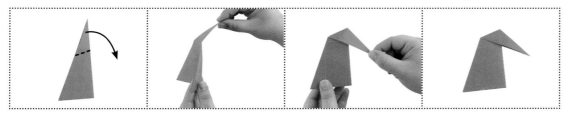

Rabbit ear folds are formed by bringing two edges of a point together using existing fold lines. The new point is folded to one side.

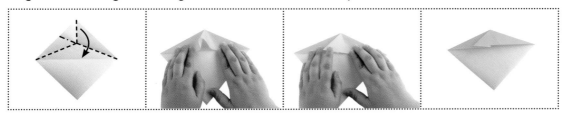

Pleat folds are made by using both a mountain fold and a valley fold.

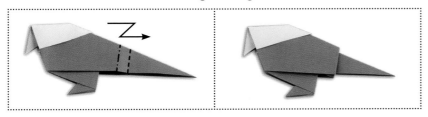

Symbols

Fold the paper in the direction of the arrow.	Fold the paper and then unfold it.	Fold the paper behind.
Turn the paper over, or rotate the paper.	Pleat the paper by reverse folding twice.	Inflate the model by blowing air into it.

★ Finch

This simple bird looks like the finches seen hopping around bird feeders or perching on fences. Try out different double-sided papers to change the look of your origami finches.

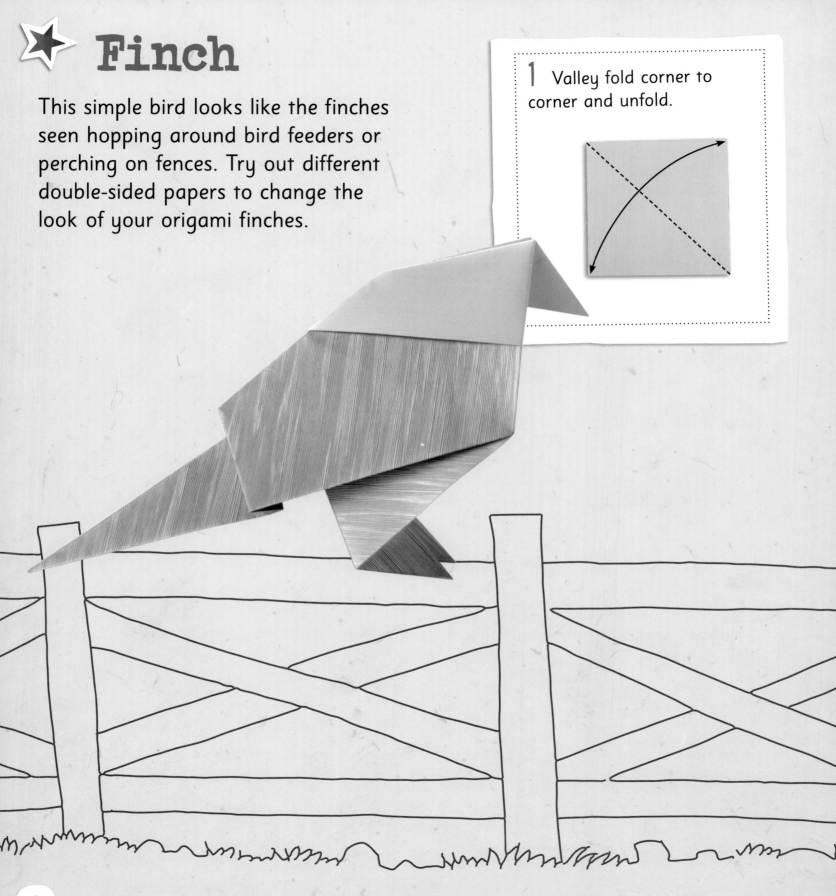

1 Valley fold corner to corner and unfold.

2 Valley fold the edges to the center.

3 Mountain fold the corner.

4 Valley fold the corners to the center and unfold.

5 Squash fold the corners using the creases made in step 4.

6 Valley fold the points.

7 Valley fold the model in half.

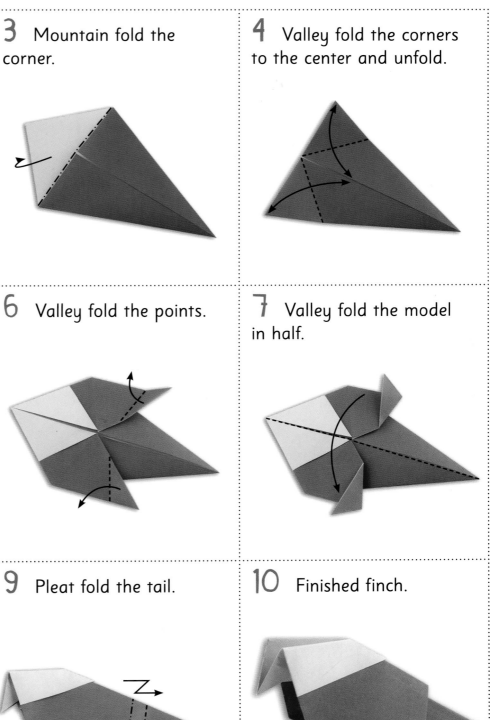

8 Inside reverse fold the point to form a beak.

9 Pleat fold the tail.

10 Finished finch.

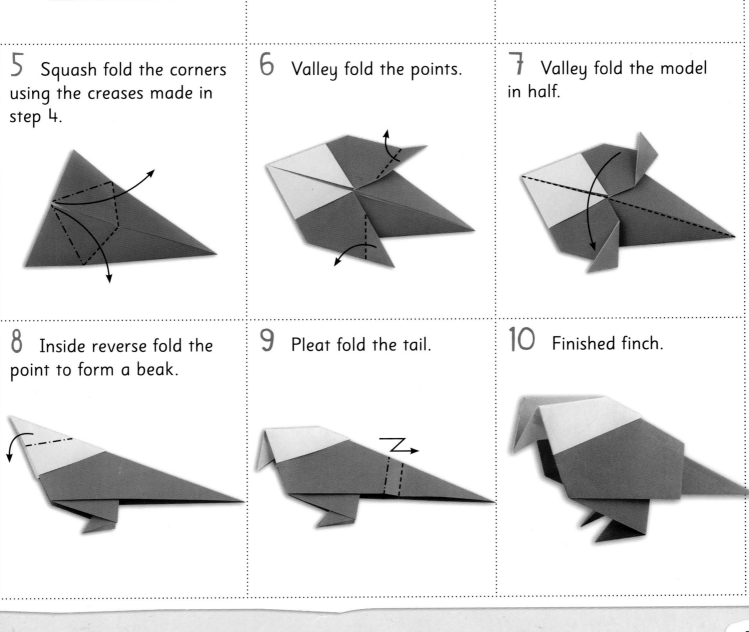

Bluebell

Bluebell stems droop under the weight of their beautiful blossoms. Fold a bouquet of these bell-shaped flowers to brighten someone's day.

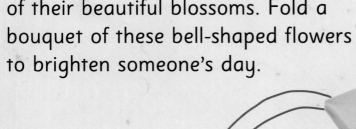

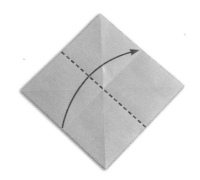

1 Valley fold corner to corner in both directions and unfold.

2 Valley fold edge to edge and unfold.

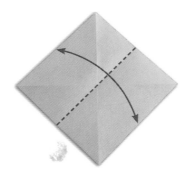

3 Valley fold edge to edge.

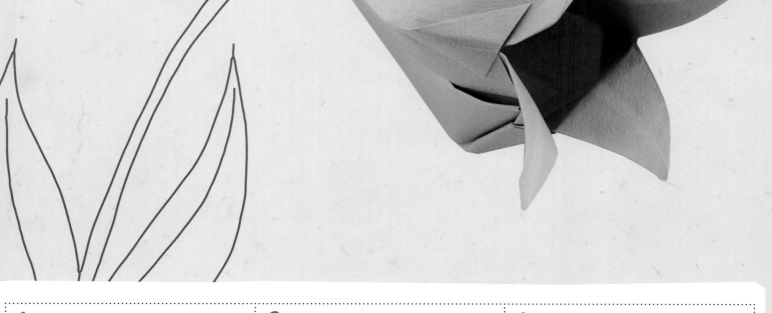

4 Squash fold.

5 Valley fold the top flaps to the center. Repeat behind.

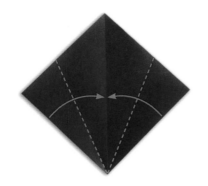

6 Valley fold the top flaps to the center. Repeat behind.

7 Squash fold the top flaps. Repeat behind.

8 Mountain fold the top flaps. Repeat behind.

9 Curl the points down to make petals.

10 Push out the center of the model with your finger.

11 Finished bluebell.

Ninja Star

This four-point star looks like the throwing stars made famous by Japanese ninjas. Tap into your inner ninja with just two pieces of paper.

Unit #1

1 Valley fold edge to edge in both directions and unfold.

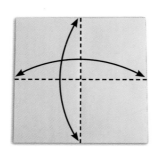

2 Valley fold the edges to the center.

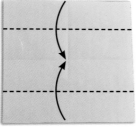

3 Valley fold edge to edge.

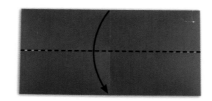

4 Valley fold the corners to the edges.

5 Valley fold the edges to the center crease.

6 Turn the unit over.

7 Finished unit #1. Set aside.

8 Valley fold edge to edge in both directions and unfold.

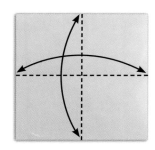

9 Valley fold the edges to the center.

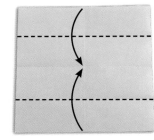

10 Valley fold edge to edge.

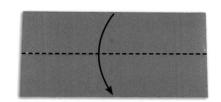

11 Valley fold the corners to the edges.

12 Valley fold the edges to the center crease.

13 Finished unit #2.

14 Lay unit #2 on top of unit #1.

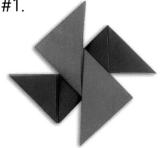

15 Valley fold the points of unit #1 and tuck them into the pockets of unit #2.

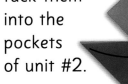

16 Turn the model over.

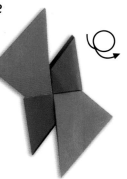

17 Valley fold the points of unit #2 and tuck them into the pockets of unit #1.

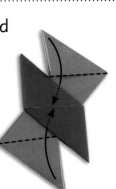

18 Finished ninja star.

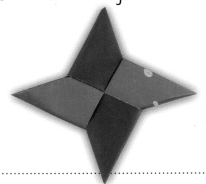

Baubles and Garland

Decorate any tree with an array of garland and baubles. Origami bluebells, finches, and ninja stars offer endless possibilities for wonderful hanging and perched ornaments.

Ninja Star Ornament

What You Need

scissors

origami ninja star

6-inch (15-centimeter) long
   piece of string

*fold the ninja star from
   6-inch (15-cm) squares

What You Do

1 Cut a small notch out of the folded edge of one point of the ninja star. Make the notch slightly below the tip of the point.

2 Thread the string though the hole created by the notch.

3 Tie the ends of the thread into a knot. Pull the string so the knot hides inside the star's point.

4 Hang your ninja star ornament.

Perched Bird

What You Need

origami finch

craft glue

wooden clothespin

*fold the finch from a
6-inch (15-cm) square

What You Do

1 Spread the feet of the finch apart slightly.

2 Glue the clothespin inside of the center of the finch. Position the clothespin so it opens just below the finch's feet.

3 When the glue dries, clip your perched bird to a tree branch.

Bluebell Garland

What You Do

1 Cut small leaf shapes out of the green sheet of paper. Make twice as many leaves as you have bluebells.

2 Stretch out the string and space the bluebells evenly along its entire length.

3 With an adult's help, use hot glue to attach the points of each bluebell to the string. Finish each blossom by gluing a leaf to each side of each flower.

4 After the glue cools, hang the bluebell garland anywhere you like to add a touch of spring to any room.

What You Need

scissors

sheet of green paper

4 or more origami bluebells

24-inch (61-cm) long or longer piece of string

hot glue gun

*fold the bluebells from
6-inch (15-cm) squares

Photo Frame

Showcase your wallet-size photos with stunning photo frames. For the perfect size, fold this model with a 6-inch (15-cm) square of paper.

1 Valley fold edge to edge and unfold.

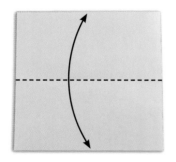

2 Valley fold the edges to the center.

3 Valley fold edge to edge and unfold.

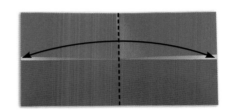

4 Valley fold the edges to the center and unfold.

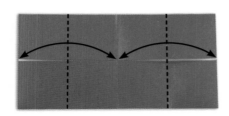

5 Valley fold the edge to the creases made in step 4 and unfold.

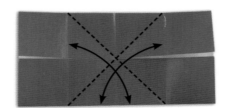

6 Squash fold on the existing creases.

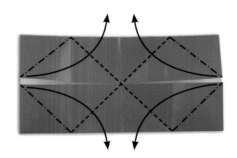

7 Valley fold the inside edges of each flap to the center.

8 Squash fold all four points.

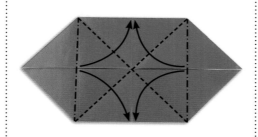

9 Valley fold the edges of each of the four squares to their center creases.

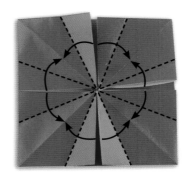

10 Squash fold all of the triangles.

11 Valley fold all four points.

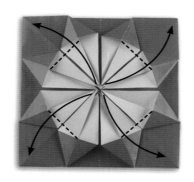

12 Valley fold all four points.

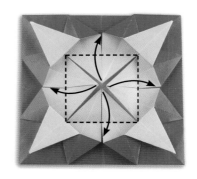

13 Place a wallet-size photo inside the frame.

14 Finished photo frame.

Photo Frame Ornament

Here's an ornament that looks great no matter which way the breeze blows. Front or back, this double-sided photo frame always shows you a face you adore.

What You Need

2 origami photo frames

double-sided tape

2 wallet-size photos

12-inch (30.5 cm) long piece of string

*fold the photo frames from 6-inch (15-cm) squares

What You Do

1 Decide how you would like your photo frames to line up and hang back-to-back. Frames could line up perfectly or be offset. They could also hang like a square or a diamond.

2 Tape the photos inside the frames based on the orientation you decided on in step 1. Set aside.

3 Tie the two ends of the string together in a knot.

4 Apply tape to the back of one photo frame. Place the knotted part of the string on the tape near the center of the frame.

5 Place the back of the second photo frame on top of the tape and the string. Be sure the frames line up the way you decided in step 1 and press firmly.

6 Hang the ornament from a tree branch, a light fixture, or anywhere it can turn freely.

Paper Crane

The paper crane may be the most well-known origami model in the world. Legend says folding 1,000 of these paper birds brings good luck.

1 Valley fold corner to corner in both directions and unfold. Turn the paper over.

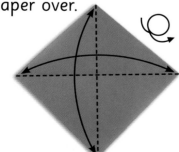

2 Valley fold edge to edge and unfold.

3 Valley fold edge to edge.

4 Squash fold.

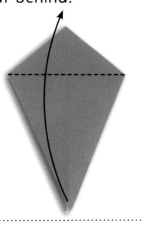

5 Valley fold the top flaps to the center and unfold. Repeat behind.

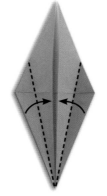

6 Inside reverse fold the top flaps. Repeat behind.

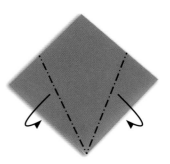

7 Valley fold the top flap. Repeat behind.

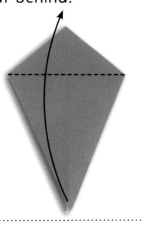

8 Valley fold the top flaps to the center crease. Repeat behind.

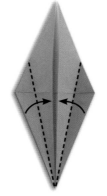

9 Inside reverse fold the points upward.

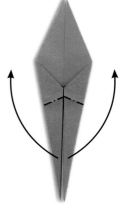

10 Inside reverse fold the point to make the head.

11 Gently pull the wings down and apart.

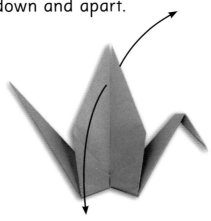

12 Finished crane.

Three-Crane Ornament

Take origami ornaments to new heights! By simply threading classic paper cranes on a string, you'll send them soaring. No matter where it hangs, this ornament will delight anyone who sees it!

What You Need

20-inch (51-cm) long piece of string

3 origami cranes

large sewing needle

bead

*fold the cranes from 6-inch (15-cm) squares

What You Do

1 Tie a loop in one end of the string.

2 Thread the other end of the string through the eye of the sewing needle.

3 Push the needle through the center of an origami crane's back. Pull the needle and string out of the bottom of the crane.

4 Remove the needle and tie a knot just below the crane to hold it in place.

5 Repeat steps 2–4 with the other two cranes. Space the cranes evenly along the string.

6 Tie a bead on the end of the string to finish the three-crane ornament.

Read More

Sjonger, Rebecca. *Maker Projects for Kids Who Love Paper Engineering.* Be a Maker. New York: Crabtree Publishing Company, 2016.

Song, Sok. *Everyday Origami: A Foldable Fashion Guide.* Fashion Origami. North Mankato, Minn.: Capstone Press, 2016.

Turnbull, Stephanie. *Paper Crafts.* Try This! Mankato, Minn.: Smart Apple Media, 2016.

Ventura, Marne. *Awesome Paper Projects You Can Create.* Imagine It, Build It. North Mankato, Minn.: Capstone Press, 2016.

Internet Sites

FactHound offers a safe, fun way to find Internet sites related to this book. All of the sites on FactHound have been researched by our staff.

Here's all you do:
Visit *www.facthound.com*
Type in this code: 9781515735861

Super-cool stuff! Check out projects, games and lots more at www.capstonekids.com